IN THE HAPPY VALLEY

Also by Tony Connor

With Love Somehow (1962)
Lodgers (1965)
Kon in Springtime (1968)

TONY CONNOR

IN THE HAPPY VALLEY

POEMS

LONDON
OXFORD UNIVERSITY PRESS
NEW YORK TORONTO
1971

Oxford University Press, Ely House, London W. 1
GLASGOW NEW YORK TORONTO MELBOURNE WELLINGTON
CAPE TOWN SALISBURY IBADAN NAIROBI DAR ES SALAAM LUSAKA ADDIS ABABA
BOMBAY CALCUTTA MADRAS KARACHI LAHORE DACCA
KUALA LUMPUR SINGAPORE HONG KONG TOKYO

S.B.N. 19 211806 4

PRINTED IN GREAT BRITAIN BY
THE BOWERING PRESS, PLYMOUTH

FOR

NINA TOLL

CONTENTS

ACKNOWLEDGEMENTS

ACKNOWLEDGEMENTS are due to the editors of *Ambit*, *Critical Quarterly*, *Denver Quarterly*, *Michigan Quarterly Review*, and *Phoenix*, in which a few of these poems have previously appeared.

AUTHOR'S NOTE

THESE poems of disease, death, and regeneration were written—for the most part—in the U.S.A., where I lived for two years from 1967 to 1969. The Happy Valley may be understood as both a Realty Man's phantasy of the area of New England in which I had my home, and the valley of Ezekiel's vision, whose bones were not without the chance of new life.

NEW PLACE

MUFFLING our gasps of lust
trucks without mufflers
shift gear on Route 9.

Their headlights sweep the room;
we are two thrashing
ghosts as they rend past
going somewhere as fast
as the country road
will allow.
                    We lie back,
going nowhere, waiting
in dense black
for the next truck's passing.
Our foreign white flesh
on the all-American
maplewood floor resists
every parable I begin.
In the approaching roar
shadows shape and lengthen.

Here there are new rules
to be learned. We appear,
disappear, appear, as the night cools.

WALKING BY BIRCHWOODS

THE moon like a slippery secret
comes clear of the humped hills.

I am returning from the laundromat
thinking about the dead,
as though that watched turbulence of cleansing
had dislodged discreet spirits.

The least of them knows me too well;
some of them are my spitting image
and kick the snowbanks as I do,
whistling the latest tunes through clenched teeth.

Not that they come to accuse;
merely to remind in Massachusetts.

My old amiable companions;
insulted, hurt, ignored—no matter,
they are glad to see me doing so well:
for whom else did they die?

My burden is children's clothes in pillowcases.

See those shimmering shapes dismember
at the first car's headlights!
Into the dark woods they scurry:
dried snow blown by the night wind.

The moon follows me mildly down the valley.

THE TEA PARTY

THREE old ladies sit on my porch.
They smile shyly, uncertainly,
as I emerge from the house with a briefcase.
I am a clever and successful young man.

Their talk is of rape, and reincarnation,
and of many things that have happened to them;
what world I stride to they cannot guess,
but my kindness is enough to give them ease.

I glance back,
                    they lean together with secrets—
even cruel lovers scented with lavender,
                                        memories
unfolded neatly from drawers long locked,
                                        trinkets
old ladies care for.

I walk away to my work; they are part
of a late afternoon in Indian Summer.
I imagine them as aging with the day,
                                        to fade gently away
before my return, before the moon rises
over the maples.
                    As though benevolence need not be crazed
by spite and impatience at lingering death.

THEME AND AFFIRMATION

I

How positive the pen appears
moving across the paper it changes!
The mind, cautiously considering its realities,
takes heart, and stranger metaphors, from the act.
To deal with words—which are, in a sense,
the trees of Connecticut roaring outside the house,
black windy night, the house with me within it,
and all of this within the mind invented to make the poem—
is to despise, for trickery, one's own eloquence.

One has tried the silence of writing nothing,
without success.
                    Brilliant, brilliant,
the wordless poems of winter walks,
of days without food,
of neighbours' labours on snowclogged cars.
Beautifully apposite the conjunctions
of distant assassins and cornflake packets
your children spill on the kitchen floor.

To write it down is to bring to judgement
the wholesome invisibilities of the imagination . . .
in a sense.
               Innocence is not to be strived for,
though perhaps it can be arrived at;
and not by refusing the clumsy confusing act
of breaking the perfect-making silence.

II

THE boots stand under the table
waiting to move.
                    They lack human feet
but that is no impediment.

I see them twitching, hesitating
in a little shuffle;

which direction shall they take?

If they march purposefully forth
into the night other boots will join them.

They could stamp everything out.
No force on earth is equipped to fight boots.

They could stamp everything out.

A world of boots!
The end of poems,
polite conversation,
naked concord,
political argument,
children's games.

But their time has not come.
They tiptoe from the room,
along the corridor,
and into the right cupboard.

I shall wear them in the morning.

GOOD TIMES

THERE are days when the world
welcomes you in.

The landscape lies open;
the people, noticing
and unnoticing of you,
are alike in making you known.

A curse has been lifted, you could believe;
momentarily, it is true, in the scale of things—
but lifted.
            You go about happy but puzzled
                                                naked-chilled
smiling into the voracious laughter of your youngest child.

FLU AT THE SHERATON-CHICAGO

CHANNELS of smudgy faces
ride upon the one unvarying voice:

Bad breath bad guys deodorants and death.

The bulk-bought furniture,
the personalized paintings, the selection of magazines
in the rack lie stunned in the room's heat.

If I force the venetian blinds
in a sudden panic, I will sense through aimless dense
snow the real world.
                    Metropolis where the judgements
of commerce take grey desirable shape.

Out in the dark
the Great polluted Lake crackles its icy fringe.
Slender white horizontals thicken upon the skeleton
of the tallest apartment block in the world.

My pill is like a parody of the bright spot:
the last embarrassed girl or the last corpse
being flushed away.
                    I gulp it down.

My sleep is haunted by the faithless multitudes of America.

ANOTHER ENDING

My coat on the door
looks as if it's been finally
vacated. A dead man's.
I can't make anything happen.
My children love me
and I don't care.
My comb is full of falling hair.

That face in the mirror
won't bear looking at;
I write letters to women who
never knew me and to
others who can't have me.
I imagine slow paralysis
beginning like this.

In dreams people knock
at doors I can't open;
I rush to doors where nobody knocked.
When I burn the garbage
an icy full moon wobbles
wildly in waves of heat
from the blaze at my feet.

I smile and fulfil my contract.
Courteous and even gay,
at parties I do not know
myself. And when eternity
yawns again, threatening
to stop the throat the breath,
I concentrate on death.

THE ATTACK

INTO the mind's emptiness
come thoughts of sickness:
the body, the brain choking—
agony-end of everything.

Consciousness narrows;
the pounding heart's slow blows
assume midnight; the room
throbs like a struck drum.

There is nothing, nothing at all
to be done—the attack is fatal.
Ears whine, nausea drags
sideways, beneath wild legs

the floor shakes; full moon's face
is a doctor helpless,
watching nerves sever
eyes go out mouth slaver.

Then you are back, complete,
not knowing the half of it,
but magically healed
to a ponderous night-world

of cricket and frog sounds,
far wars and near wounds,
while sundry small thoughts purr
into a certain future.

Something has won something,
for what it is worth. Your strong
being prowls through the house.
The moon is anonymous.

SQUARED BY WALLS

from the Hungarian of László Nagy

Couldn't you have died,
or at least bled,
instead of pacing the floor
stunned with despair?
You kept clear of the trouble—
bullets, armoured tracks, emblazoned
girls' screams. Not for you broken
wheels, scattering rooftiles,
grim gangs of working lads,
and soot-brindled petals.
You did not spill one drop
of blood, and when it stopped,
you had only gone grey and mad.

In usual winter weather
you stand here; no other
but yourself, and wide awake,
squared by walls that echo
a cough like raking
gunfire. It's not merely
your flesh that's cold;
mind and heart are frozen—crowned
by knives of ice.
You are ashamed of your melting phrases;
as if you had lost the right
to think of spring
and lilacs—the lung-like trees blossoming.
What agony for a Lord of Life!
Yet deep in the secret places
of your being, furtive with guilt,
you are breathing on the frosted pane:
beginning to look at the world again.

ROOM WITH INSECT

In a lonely room at night
the buzz in my head flies out
embodied as a busy insect.
It bounces against windowpanes,
it zig-zags from wall to wall
from ceiling to carpet,
disappearing momentarily in shadows.

My brain clears;
I seem about to define
whatever it is I wish to concentrate on.

But the insect begins to die.
It slips from the ruby eye
of the Mexican God above the fireplace,
it drags its torpid body across my desk.

I summon it home in fright

disembody it quickly

and lie awake trembling all night.

LISTENING TO BACH IN FRANKLIN COUNTY

The police in the cities prepare for summer,
there is much talk of the need for order.

A fugue in the wilderness
ravishes the hearts of a few impotent men.
With lunatic fastidiousness
the music steps from my window
towards the scrub forest before
and the Shopping Plaza behind,

inviting assassination—
such fervent benevolence open to the night air.

It all happens again.
                    The just go down,
the greedy, the stupid;
                    battlefields
become the pastures of scholars.

One thinks of ways to preserve one's sanity . . .
fugues whose structure one only senses,
a political sticker on the windshield
that partly obscures one's vision.

The forfeiture of giant miseries
                              to write
a small poem at midnight.

IN THE HAPPY VALLEY

I

It is warm but the body shivers.

Caught in admiring glances
the mind cramps in invisible ice.

Everywhere looks like nowhere.

II

I smile at people I meet,
enquiring of small matters
they are flattered to have remembered,
but my hands are growing hairy
I turn away my face.
                    Come moonrise
I may be in the westward forests
that grow to Canada:
a werewolf snarling impotently
beyond the perimeters of lights
that distinguish Esso stations.

At dawn I shall slouch home,
courteous as ever,
looking for things to do.

III

A child does a drawing of me
                    and rubs it out.
I walk twice around the supermarket
purchasing nothing.
                    Clapping hands
are great flightless birds in a nightmare.

IV

THIS is a fertile valley.
On good days I study the range of hills
that lies like a melting woman
five miles to the south.

Brown fields emerging from snow,
sombre clumps of pines,
feathery dustings of naked birches,
unending drifts of slow smoke
from a hidden dump,
and beyond them all the snow-scored slidden thighs and breasts
and head half buried in the plain
milleniums ago.

V

WHAT use if the penis ache and the mind tremble?
She was never the one who stands with dustpan and brush,
or statuesquely arranged for an evening out

done with me before I began.

VI

To identify anguish
                    and then to dignify.
Who knows what might stop
my heartbeat shaking the bed
in the latest Great Nation?

Should I march on the Capitol,
or offer myself piece by piece
to the electrically operated garbage disposer
beneath the sink,
'which actually benefits by being fed bones'?

VII

THE spirit that wants to die
is quickened by fantasies of sickness . . .

The skull crushed to mitherless black.

Stones have been men.

VIII

THE negritude of imagined ancestors . . .
photographed ones who went insane,
or disappeared conspicuously forever,
or whose names are brought to mind only with effort,
glow with faint green light
as I check unanxiously water oil amps revs miles,
and the turnpike goes on and on in the headlights:
a silent film made by a maniac.

To familiar places I do not know.
Foreign confusions of towns and shires.

IX

IN a windy graveyard,
humble with flaking slate and crumbled words,
I am shown where the poet of the place
is murmurously remembered.

Her epitaph touches silence,
and shyly withdraws into the world of Variorums
and such as we who come to her one day.

It is not the wind that wobbles me.
Someone
is walking on my grave.
Myself on mine?
I am starting to thaw at last.

X

WITH pleasure the self recalls its purpose:
so foolish . . .
Just to go on and on
gathering news of death.

Children growing
taking and giving
The old staring through windows
as the latest Chevrolets purr past
Food and its evacuation
Bills overdrafts
the inventions of wealth
Cunts like brainless hands
taking and giving
Mountains of human hair
spectacles and false teeth
in ludicrous abundance
Underpaid invoice clerks
Bosses who get drunk often
or take up chess
The admission that you
that you
have inherited the earth.

XI

So. Because. Therefore. Maybe.
Beautiful boys my door is open, at least,
and what you can take is yours.
Touch my tweeds—
they are good to the hand,
but like my words
heal nothing.
Would Keats have sought me out?
I doubt it.
All of you look like Keats.

XII

REMEMBER my house as an old house . . .
twisting passages, dark stairways,
many empty rooms.
                                        Going to bed
the children frighten themselves with werewolves.
They are unaccustomed to forests
and furry things that creep humpbacked
from the trees at twilight
to prise the lids off garbage cans
with delicate paws.
                                        I tell them werewolves
went with the dragons.
                                        Racoons are nice.
I scoff at werewolves.

XIII

EVERYTHING is speech, and plain at that,
if I can make it so.
                                        And yet . . . .
How to suggest an only way of looking?
Through blind eyes at the back of a poem's head?

What deadly or joyful season lacks its lies.

XIV

ICE is spongy on the pond
at the forest's edge.
                                        A few wild flowers are out.
The body shivers acceptable response
to a wind that is still winter's.

Moving again, the mind in its distresses
hopes without reason, bearing guilt
for crimes only its dead could name.

To the manner born.

If only to spank with laughter a puddling child
if only to chase a squirrel
or admire a bomber's sleek shape in the blue,
if only to clasp one loving woman's hand
in lieu of the dead
you could not bring yourself to touch.

The hills look kindly.

AMONG STUDENTS

TYRES squeal at the corner
as car after car
is yanked round too fast.
                                        Young men
are at their games with death.

On the Fraternity lawns
they bound and whoop,
slinging footballs to one another,
crashing to earth without thought.

I walk among them,
glad I am too old to be impressed
into the youthful phantasies
of elderly politicians; glad
I am still alive to watch my firm flesh failing.

Soon it will not be worth offering
to anything more dramatic
than a life's work.

IN THE LOCKER ROOM

EVERYTHING's clean and jolly:
genitals, butt, and belly
show with a nakedness
that causes none distress.
Between the locker rows
heaps of abandoned clothes
lie like a beaten race
crumpled in its disgrace.
All's cheer above—the Lords
of muscle-power and words
tingling from gym and joke
relax for a quick smoke.
Glad to be back again
in this clear world of men
I banish from my mind
the dark thoughts of its kind.
I rub my itching balls.
The seed of criminals
and maniacs waits
in those hanging fruits.

TEMPTATIONS OF THE WORLD

First heard,
they are the heavy boots of a stranger
on your stairs at 3 a.m.
You awake, heart racing
from a dream,
and it *is* a dream.

At noon your dead father
speaks from across a table,
saying 'You know you should not have done that'
—the words you are reading
that moment
on the page of a novel.

The radio reports
assassinations, riots,
real bullets in real flesh.
Colour television
gives you the true babyburning quality of the fires.

You have good reason to fear strangers.

There are many things you should not have done.

But you were battered to death
long since in dreams

and your father does not know
you are even thinking about America.

ON THE PENINSULA

THE difficult climbs are best.
The terrain
thwarts Democracy in places.

On the easier slopes sportsmen on motorbikes
ingeniously adapted to withstand the strains
imposed by mountains roar up and down.

In the lower campgrounds
tents like houses loom beside
the latest automobiles.
Gas-ranges, refrigerators,
and toilets function perfectly in trailers
trade-named Navajho, Pathfinder, Trailblazer.

The discoverers of the region
called the mountains The Olympics,
gave settlements
classical titles.
Sappho still holds—
though a dump of cheap compound houses and junked cars.

Psyche has become *Pish*.

HUNTING THE GOEDUCK

UNLIKELY as its name, it is descried initially
as an abrupt vertical squirt out of wet sand
at very low tide.
Its body lies three feet below;
its squirting neck retracts at the aproaching footfall
of hunters (on the rare occasions when the observer
of the squirt, his eye fixed bulging
as he squelches forward crushing small crabs
and shouting his companion,
gets anywhere near and does not end up
on an empty stretch of beach
damning his delusive eyesight).

I have evidence
that a stockbroker and a poet, together,
may hunt it unsuccessfully for three hours,
with the morning sun expanding above the Pacific,
and a day neither knows what to do with lying ahead.

The stockbroker tossing his emptied beercans
into the shallows.
The poet peeved by ludicrous metaphors.

THE HAMA HAMA RIVER ROAD

It is partly the effort of the climb
that numbs the brain.
                    'Not a route, but a track'
dragging the body upward through forest;
2000 feet in the first mile with worse to come.

Gigantic mossed rocks like wet sponges
swell in the fetid stillness of the rain forest,
then, as the trees thin,
naked rock utters from unrhetorical crevices
daintily bobbing alpine flowers,
                              torrents
spume rainbows above foaming pools.

Beauty is not a word you would say, if you had the breath.

Once on the unobstructed mountainside
you may gaze across the valley at the dazzle
of higher peaks,
            or up to where,
a few feet ahead, the first snow
lies in an everlasting shadow.
                        You care
in retrospect.
        The second mile, nothing matters
except not giving in.
            And when you reach there—
there where the turquoise water of the tarn
spills gently from its volcanic hollow
as it did before Man—mountain goats
clatter away, staring from a distance

with eyes like the dead.

CONVALESCENCE

THE dead speak a strange tongue.
It is like the shimmering trill
of tree-frogs and crickets
crossed by the rush from nowhere into nowhere
of unseen cars.
In fact that's what it is.

The streetlighting is stupidly patient
in small towns late at night;
I walk abroad
in my abundant agonies, giving it something to do.

After near-death
one thinks to meet walking spirits;
to be buttonholed into ultimate mysteries
beneath the slightly stirring maples
seems almost deserved.

A policeman
watches me warily.
A dog sniffs,
and follows for half a block.

The usual silent commotion deep in space
shines on my multipli-lacerated scalp,
beneath which
I trim my expectations.

THE LAST TIME

IT will be a day in broad winter,
probably in a foreign though familiar place
with a continent pressing the back of my head
like an unidentifiable preoccupation
three thousand miles deep.
There will be students in the streets below,
hurrying to classes, and some few dawdling
to talk of demonstrations.
                                        The newspapers
that day will contain carefully documented reports
of the latest space flights, the problems
of disadvantaged minorities in the cities,
and second-hand accounts of vaguely miraculous births,
fashions, genocide, political upheavals,
and so on, in other parts of the world.

There will be snow falling onto the snow
already thick on the ground.
                                        It will be falling steadily,
but not so thickly that I cannot see
from my high window the frozen river
beyond the town, and beyond that the casual sprawl
of the mental hospital.
                                    My mind
will have been turning for hours upon my obligations
to the living and the dead, with a bearable sense
of its own inadequacy.
                                    My shoulders
will be aching, and perhaps one leg.

The time will be afternoon, before the light starts to go.

It is possible that I will be thinking,
                                                        at that moment,

of my wife's beauty and failings, or of my children
as they take on the world in small, touching ways—
like staying over with friends.
                                                I will find myself
shredding paper; I will see the white flakes
falling from hand to desk.
                                        I will raise my eyes
to the window and confirm what I know:

There are empty comments everywhere.

I will have written my last poem.

TRAVELLER'S RETURN

DOUBLE talking devils of illness arrive
in the bodies of shameless debtor friends.

They pretend, pretend they owe nothing,
tickling your sullen spirit with scandalous gossip
and tales told in your absence.
                                        Now your brain
roars like a thunder sheet. Now your limbs tremble
and your hair comes out in handfuls.
                                                Dream-doctors
tell of kidney failure. You see your astral body
devoured by housedogs.

You are back where you belong, breathes the arse of a sycophant.
Relax, relax, mutter the milkbottles.

So this is home, you think to the mirror,
pulling out forgotten treasures
from the backs of drawers.

DEMONSTRATIONS OF AFFECTION

I

In dreams
I have seen you for what you are:
the mouth of Hell,
a cunt agape to receive the damned.

Laughing
you remind me too.
You are going to engulf me,
of that I am sure.

No wonder you must fondle me often
No wonder you must kiss me for nothing
No wonder you must reiterate how much you love me.

Being the unwilling possessor
of such deadly orifices.

II

You have not heard me.
Again
you have not heard me.

One day I shall speak
with Godlike crashes
from my
black clouds.
Lightning will shrivel the children,
the kitchen floor will split
revealing
corpses I have not decided on yet.

I'll give you something
to pretend ignorance of.

III

You have gone to bed, tightlipped and elegant—
as to your death before me.

I sit listening to a Mozart quintet,
trying to invent a girl I first heard it with.

IV

It is a long time since we spoke
to each other in simple terms.
Now it is difficult, unless one—waking
before the world assumes its weight—
catches the other murmuring in sleep
and, thinking little of it, answers
from a mind unpondering.
                                        By day
our sentences rake to the world's end,
as though there were nothing
each had not a stake in the other would not steal.

You say 'I threw that broken box away.'
My grunt knows the enormity of the act.

V

Wiping
the smell of women
from my hands
and loins,
I am fidgety with words.

In the upper darkness
her sleep
has already begun.

Wordlessly it flows
through the house
oozing my juices.

VI

VETERAN of many wars,
how you confuse me.
Your apparent guilelessness
leads me to a gunpoint.
And when I am taken prisoner
you protest ignorance;
'That's your idea' you say,
'I don't even have a cheque-book.'

'Such sophistry' I think
as I visit other women.
By your casual magnanimity
set free.

A LADY IN A POEM

A GREY Middletown day,
no time or place for extremes, perhaps.
Everybody making an easy show
of being everybody; the afternoon
succumbing without struggle.

But she, all alone only she,
is expensive-fur-hat deep in phantasy:
choppered her husband falls dead,
and so, and so . . . father, friends, neighbours,
herself! split from head to toe!

She hovers, lost, recovers and
sees the broad river winking
by no means broadly in bland
collusion across Main Street's
going-some-place traffic. Is it a trick?—

like her husband's double,
with suave wobble resurrected
to approach whispering sweet
nothings into the giggling ear
of an arrow-straight-legged co-ed?

Of course. She must rehearse
the bold bare phantasies of this verse,
as Sears Roebuck's closes
and—lacking forbearance—
the poet makes his appearance
bowing, and handing her a bunch of roses.

MAKING LOVE HALF-ASLEEP

WHOSE hands are these questing
my body? There is a face
I do not know forming
against mine. My arms embrace

flesh and it is demanding
of me—the alien stink
swilling my brain, rending
the dream in which I think

clearly and fast. I squeeze
it dully, and enter it with
fingers that cannot choose,
and I am riding wrath,

stirring the turmoil's centre,
in the furious howl
of the storm I am a splinter
stuck in the blackest bowel

of creation. I am going to be dead,
surely: smothered, fused
with a monster cold-blooded
and lecherous, violent in its crazed

appetites. Afterwards,
lying drained and chilled,
I know what we are; but words
will not serve. I hold

your hand, and we are home
my poor silent companion,
watching ourselves become
man and wife again.

KAREN'S DREAM

She woke from things eating one another
and he was beside her as he had always been
a face neither young nor old and resembling
how many children tucked into kinder darkness
somewhere below. She stroked his mouth
and his cheek and the dull glow
where his frontal lobes bumped the close air.
He did not wake and might never wake perhaps
only in an outer layer of dream sleeping there
between an evening she could not remember and
unimaginable dawn. She touched him beneath the sheets
unmoving his privates slack as a corpse's
she touched her own body and her scars were braille
of a dead language she could not read.
Conversations in restaurants returned to her
anniversaries at the theatre windy days
on high moors visits from parents but she was
inventing them. Her eyes came back
from the darkness with no furniture and her ears
brought back no tick tock and she was alone
of course in bed and then the bed had gone
and she was almost nothing and she thought
about nothing and the thought stopped
and the things had eaten one another.

AUTUMNALS

I

A PLAGUE of dying wasps;
the laying-down of tigerish small malevolences
on window ledges and in bowls of standing water.

Children come kicking leaves from school.
In the folds of women's smiles I see summer
creeping from its last place.

As if all things were ending
I encumber myself with remembered pleasures;
from crammed dreams I try not to wake,
my days are inert with dead happiness.

II

LET the postman come with his handfuls
of engaging testimonials from distant friends
whose words stir the chemical air of two continents.

Let the doctor come with final messages
from the concentration camps: prescriptions for Librium.

Let the dustbinmen come to prove
that civilization still endures.

III

THE thunder is a brain-bruise
throbbing.   Throbbing
on no words. The lightning
shows one red rose
staring in through the window
blind as a bloodstain.

When the rain comes
it heals the bruise
and batters flat the rose.

I speak of the death of love.

IV

PAST travel agencies alight with winter offers
and dress shops showing the latest hemline
a guttering world goes.

The elegiacs of functional disorder.

The poisoning of a nimble tongue.

V

AN after-breakfast ghost
above the still flowering parkbeds.
A child's question: 'Is the moon famous?'

Beside the stink of a Domesday stream
where it slinks from a culvert.

VI

INTENSE but diffuse like voices arguing
in a foreign language through a wall.

Portentous but without meaning
like the room you wake to.

Rock-hard but porous
like your sense of yourself.

Inviting but rejecting
like the black cone of the night sky.

Meanwhile I nod to strangers,
pat the flanks of dogs,
and hold imaginary conversations
with the comradely shrunken heads of conkers.

VII

THERE is always good reason to say Goodbye,
to retake possession of absence—
for you maintain your shadow with effort
and your books ignore you.
See! The mirrors are ready to let you go forever.
Your name is impatient to be forgotten.

NAMES ON STONE

In old graveyards
I could wonder what matters.
All those particular names
affect me like a starry sky.

Who was a good man?
Who cheated many?
Who greeted each day with a song?
Whose life was one long pain?

Tumours, palsies,
hare-lips, hunch-backs,
are gone with kindness
and the odour of sanctity.

Some evidence of riches remains,
and of poverty; but both
soon become part
of the same official care.

If you go back far enough
even the most stubborn accumulations
lose all meaning.
Stones hold names

like stars. You look,
and around you
the emptiness deepens
with everything named that no one knows.

OLD MEN

WHEN there was war they went to war,
when there was peace they went to the labour exchange,
or carried hods on an hour's notice.
If their complaints were heard in Heaven
no earthly sign was given.

They have suffered obscurely a bleak recurring dream
many lifetimes long. Wounded and gassed
for noble causes they were not thought fit to understand
made idle to satisfy the greed of their betters
lectured when it suited the State
ignored when it suited the State
flattered by comedians
studied by young sociologists,
they have survived to be cosseted by the Regional Hospital Board.

They sit on a low stone wall in front of The Home
in an afternoon sun that shines like new,
grateful to have been allowed so much.

They puff black pipes.
Their small eyes see dead wives and children who emigrated.
They talk about the evening meal
and that old bugger George who's going senile.

When they walk in they tread gingerly,
not trusting the earth to stay beneath them for much longer.

THREE ENCOUNTERS

I

My darling with the dark eyes,
and fortune to patronize
incorruptible poets,
I imagine you now. Let's
talk awhile of serious
matters. 'When you are famous . . .'
you sigh; and I 'How many
supermarkets did you say
your father owned . . .?' Oh my dear,
you were too long getting here—
we could have been so happy!
And now you are just a stray
thought to play with late at night
when marriage feels like a blight
on my soul, and all wives stupids
and all kids too many kids.

II

It is like breaking out
of a nightmare—you doubt
the innocence of your
bedroom. The furniture
still has hideous life
lingering in it—if
you don't pretend slumber
it will tear you member
from member. Foolish, of
course, to lie still and stiff,
and yet you don't arise
for ages, and your clothes
nibble you as you dress
for the day's harmlessness.

III

TIMES when the will sleeps fitfully,
disturbed by nightmares
of action. Whole days
gone, staring through windows
at traffic, or with pencil
poised above a clean
sheet of paper. Worse than
the twenty-year-old's
indolent melancholy
is this state in which I
find myself in mid-life;
for I am without 'if'
to console me, or 'when'.
She came, and has now gone.

MORNING SONG

THIS northerly light is bleak,
bedrooms should face south;
the mirror claws your cheek
like time itself; your mouth

(how often moved to kiss
its image of pretty glass?),
puckered and bloodless,
drops open on 'Alas!'.

Archaic, tragic, tall,
your strong form gathers in
from a million bedrooms all
the grief of beautiful women.

Every aging body
outraged by morning light
you don for lonely study—
symbol and anchorite.

And I, a tousled fool—
not meant to understand,
except in poems—recoil
as if from a large demand

I cannot answer, although
you don't so much as glance
towards me and my show
of sleeping ignorance.

My operatic dear,
lost in your noble part—
sombre, nude, bizarre,
no live man's sweetheart—

descend to feed the children;
assume the debased forms
from which flow affection,
abuse, domestic storms,

for these I can well gauge,
and grapple with something more
than frightened patronage
(now pretending to snore).

AFTERNOON WALK

THE edges of thoughts blur
into objects that have no meaning—
though this one is called *store*
and that one *man leaning*

against mailbox. Then
the thoughts go out completely,
only to come back on
in a split second, neatly

separated and ready to change
into every mode of sanity
conceivable—from the sponge
in Woolworths' window, to the vanity

of human wishes (by Sam
Johnson, I think, patting
my pocket where the firm
bulk lies waiting).

A hard nut to crack
is day on Main Street, any
day. At the end of the block
I try to recall my agony,

and fail. The day seems good,
with nothing in it shaken;
I nod my seemly head,
and recognize the token

as one of gratitude
for being allowed to fellow
a world I can understand—
as well as a small 'hello'

to the lady who lives next door,
now smiling, and so sending
me greetings from all out there—
not not not not not ending.